whispers from the
WINDMILL

Poems of an Oklahoma Life

Kevin L. Oakes

whispers from the
WINDMILL

Poems of an Oklahoma Life

Kevin L. Oakes

Published by: Design One Four

Typesetting: Kris Oakes

Cover Design: Emory Oakes & Kris Oakes

ISBN-13: 9798338623176

Printed in USA

Acknowledgements

Thanks to my family and friends for the encouragement and the confidence to continue writing.

Thanks to my wife Tammy for your love, support and for pushing me forward.

To my son Kris, as a graphic designer by trade, thanks for making the publishing look easy.

To my son Kason for continuing to feed God's word into our hearts.

To my mother for always listening to my poems, never criticizing, being an example and a subject of so much of my work.

To my good friend C. J. Page, thanks for being that voice of reason, encouragement and never letting me quit.

And thanks to God for giving me the words, rhymes and inspiration.

Contents

INTRODUCTION

Why I Write

Preserving precious memories
With creative words and rhymes
Can help you keep that moment
Forever etched in time

On occasion words come easy
Like a mighty rushing river
And times it takes months
For your thought pattern to deliver

But when it's finally finished
And the reader has understood
The true meaning of your thinking
It is special and it's good

Especially when you help
The reader ease their mind
No words can describe the feeling
You get down deep inside

The mere thought that your words
Had an impact on someone's day
Can make your writing worth it
No matter what they say

Never mind the subject matter
Or the style in which it's done
When words come from the heart
There's nothing that can't be won

So please enjoy these lines
From a kind and gentle soul
And if a connection is made
I've then achieved my goal

CHAPTER I

Family

Momma's Table

It seemed so large as a kid
Table cloth and chairs all around
There was always food on the table
Her love she gave to surround

We sat there each meal together
As a family it was a must
To talk about things of importance
Or anything else to discuss

For this time she had your attention
To praise or to scold or to tell
Of things she always expected
To be done and be done quite well

We now have left that large table
That table where Mom carefully set
Not only the plates the glasses and such
Her expectations were meant to be met

Three sons she saw setting at that table
One by one has left on their own
To carry on the family tradition
As she had so diligently shown

Then she saw her own dear husband
Pass on to the great ever more
She sets at the table so quiet now
Her memories are quickly restored

As she thinks of the times of when
We all set at that table and shared
Life's ups and downs as a family
She listened and reasoned and cared

But the table now seems so much smaller
As now we gather around
With us, kids and grandkids included
Thirty two loved ones is where we stand now

But the grandkids have all grown accustom
To the gravy the rolls and the pie
They all want to set at that table
Before time passes them by

Now that same table has gathered
Some notable people of fame
Like Ryan and Largent and Adams
If you don't mind the dropping of names

One thing is for sure and for certain
For cooking she's known as the best
With love and gentle persuasion
We've been privileged and so very blessed

To be able to set at this table
With a humble ever gentle ole soul
And with positive words of encouragement
Our love just continues to grow

So if you're ever in east Dewey County
In the house overlooking the river
Stop in and set at that table
You'll be blessed for the time you can give her

Dear Grandma

Dear Grandma, I never knew you
But through the years I have come to know
A small amount of who you were
As our generations come and go

I know you are my great, great Grandma
And though it doesn't matter to some
I have done my research in time
And to this place today I have come

I know not why there is no stone
To mark your life's passing to the other
If the stone was stolen or lost
But I'll respect you as my mother

No generation is left to tell your story
Only you family's markers to say
The empty grave beside them
Is where you were laid that day

It had been 100 years in January
Since you parted from this place
Without a headstone left there
You'd be lost without a trace

But here at the Kansas school cemetery
Near Choctaw Oklahoma way
I'll place this stone for you, ma'am'
And hope it's here to stay

Yes maybe someone someday
Will research their family tree and find
A long distant relative lying here
And their families that are entwined

So Grandma, I hope this stone will do
For the next generations to see
It was great fun to get to know you
As I researched our family tree

We'll catch up in the years to come
When we meet someday in heaven
Somehow, I hope you're proud
Your great, great grandson, Kevin

A Bullet for the Boys

The night was perfect for hunting
No wind, no moon, clear skies
A coon hunt was on his mind
With two Grandsons by his side

To get this chance was perfect
To teach this dying art
Of chasing down the wily coon
His knowledge to impart

Both Grandsons were young of age
Around 10 or 12 I'd guess
To get to go with Grandpa
Was a treat they both confessed

When you've hunted all your life
There's things you always do
Trust your light, trust your dogs
And bring a gun with you

This night was no exception
The gun was by his side
The barrel pointed to the floorboard
In the truck's where it would ride

The dogs had hit the trail
On a coon scent that was hot
Wasn't long before they had him
But in a tree the coon was not

Under an ole chicken house
Beneath the floor he'd went
The dogs could not get to him
No matter what time they spent

One grandson had the gun
And saw a loosened board
Used the gun to pry it up
With all his strength he poured

But he saw it was no use
Cause in the course of prying
Gun stock broke, trigger guard had too
One look there was no denying

Grandpa said let's get the dogs
And head in for the night
But loading up into the truck
Their fun turned into fright

One Grandson laid the gun down
The trigger caught the seat
With a bang the gun went off
Its destiny was complete

The bullet had hit the floorboard
Then back into Grandpa's leg
It all had happened so quickly
Forgiveness the grandson begged

"Load the dogs in the truck" he yelled
The other grandson hopped
Got the dogs into the truck
And in the back he flopped

At home they assessed the damage
The wound where the bullet had passed
The pain in his leg he was feeling
He assured them it wouldn't last

When someone accidentally shoots another
The authorities are normally sent
To investigate what really had happened
And see if there's malicious intent

But Grandpa would have none of it
That call was not to be made
To protect those boys was priority
And between us that story has stayed

But enough time has now quickly passed
And those Grandsons now are grown
But the story about that faithful night
Etched in memory so very well-known

As for that stray 22 bullet
And it's place in coon hunting lore
To the grave, Grandpa took it with him
To be revered now and for evermore

The Grin

He'd be sitting at the dining table
Intently stirring his morning cup
Pondering his work day plans
That's how Pa's day would start up

Granny would be in the kitchen
And giving him the dung hill
We would listen to her jawing at him
Wishing she would just shut up and chill

But our Pa would just sit there
Listening or ignoring or a little of both
Still stirring the sugar in his coffee
While she brought him his egg and toast

Her nagging didn't seemed to bother him
Or so to us it seemed
He'd look up from his plate and grin at us
Knowing he'd like to turn and scream

He'd visit our house on occasion
And just set in the easy chair
Watch us kids play and grin
Not saying anything without a care

He was such a kind gentle soul
His voice was seldom raised
But enough of Granny's nagging
He could quiet her and go on unfazed

I guess that's the thing that stands out
As I look back on our Pa's life
A hard working farmer rancher
A far cry from the urban city strife

He always looked old as I recall
When we were young most grownups did
Now it doesn't seem so old
As it did when we were kids

The years have passed so quickly
Since our Pa has passed away
I wonder as our grandkids look at us
Do they look at us in that same way

If they do I hope they see the good
Just as I am recalling back when
When Pa would look up from his coffee
And give us that "it's ok" grin

Aunt Isie's Biscuits

Every New Year's holiday
At lunchtime our family would go
To our uncle and aunt's house
And eat the biscuits she would throw

Now it didn't matter if you
Had just started eating or was done
With hot biscuits out of the oven
I think she threw them just for fun

And you know that place called Lamberts
In Missouri where biscuits are thrown
Aunt Isie set the standard
Long before that place was known

And the taste was nothing special
In these biscuits she delivered
Simply bought out of the can
Homemade was never considered

I now understand things better
When you're feeding more than twelve
It's quicker to open the fridge
And just get them off the shelf

You knew when you went to see her
And lunch would be prepared
You'd better be good and ready
As those biscuits flew through the air

You'd say, "No Isie, I'm finished
Couldn't eat another bite"
She'd throw a hot one anyway
Maybe doing it just for spite

And just to make her happy
We ate each and every one
Cause we knew she'd keep a throwin
Until we all were done

But I wouldn't trade a memory
Aunt Isie was one of a kind
A kind and gentle soul
A better person you'll never find

My Other Dad

When I was just around 20
A man came into my life
Just prior to my own wedding
To make my sweetheart my wife

This guy married my sweethearts mother
And took her to be his bride
A handsome, hardworking fellow
I call him Dad now with pride

As time continued for both of us
We each had new lives to share
Of those things he didn't have to do
He loved us, he taught us, he cared

He taught me of things that I couldn't
Even think about doing on my own
He gave confidence and self-assurance
The depth of it is still being shown

He taught us about Christianity
About really being into the word
Of faith there is none much stronger
When he spoke we respectfully heard

I recall when storm clouds were threatening
As our son was playing baseball
He spoke to the clouds and they heeded
They rescinded and started to fall

Faith like that comes from hearing
Of God's word without any doubt
From Copeland and Hagin he taught us
What being a Christian was all about

He was also a very hard worker
From oil rigs to teaching at school
He has the ability to do most anything
What I mean he's nobody's fool

The love that he shares is unlimited
He's always there when we need
Some help or a hug or encouragement
He speaks, we listen and he leads

The grandkids know him as Pepa
Again, he didn't have to be
They hold a special place in his heart
His love you can genuinely see

So I wrote this as a reminder
Without creating too much of a fuss
And to never take for granted
What he really means to us

Mom

Growing up with a Mom
As the primary parent
Seems strange to some
But as you look it's apparent

She was the one we looked to
For guidance and love
Things only a Mom can give
With strength from above

We lived in several places
But settled in Taloga for a spell
For us to go to school
And be close to family as well

She was a teacher by then
Putting herself through school
And a strong disciplinarian
Teaching kids to obey the rules

She had to be strong
And self-sufficient of course
She worked hard in those days
As the bread winner source

With three girls to care for
And put clothes on their backs
Her desire to do well
Was one thing she never lacked

As the boys came calling
On her three lovely girls
She was very protective
They were her whole world

And when they stepped over
And did something wrong
She wore their tails out
As their wills were all strong

And when they stayed out
In the yard with the boys
The porch light would come on
You could tell she was annoyed

She moved to Seiling to teach school
Changed her life for the good
Met the man of her dreams
Like God knew that she would

An avid fan of the kids
Watching them playing ball
Seeing them all succeed
Was her goal after all

After teaching for years
She retired and does well
Keeping busy with church
And she tries not to dwell

On how she got here
To this 80th milestone
Just a number for sure
As her age isn't shown

One thing is for certain
Her faith does not waver
With guidance from the Lord
And the strength that He gave her

Runnin' With The Ringtails

The night was dark, the wind was still
The air was crisp and cold
The dogs were loaded, the guns were too
This memory will never grow old

Dad loved to hunt, didn't matter what
A coon, a duck, a goose
He felt at ease along the creek
About to turn the dogs loose

We'd park the truck upon a hill
In case we lost our way
He'd roamed these creeks all his life
He saw at night like day

The dogs started barking, you start running
Before too long they're treed
To get there before the coon jumped out
There seemed to be a need

We get to the tree, we spot the coon
And Dad, he starts to squalling
The coon don't want any part of that
The dogs they're all a bawling

Poor ole coon don't have a chance
Once he hit the ground
Ole Judy and Roho made fast work
By the neck they grasp around

Won't turn loose till their job is done
Guess they learned this lesson well
Then chain their collar to head back home
More stories we can tell

This particular night what started out
To be cold and crisp and clear
Turned out to be overcast and windy
And nothing familiar here

We had hunted several hours
Before finding the dogs on tree
With several hills and valleys crossed
Where in the world could we be

Dad used the stars to navigate
And now the clouds were heavy
No North Star to guide the way
His memory he'd have to levy

I'd never seen him lost not once
But I could see it in his eyes
We'd traveled a little too far this time
Would this be our demise

But a kid of 12 looks up to Dad
To always find his way
The wind and cold was bad that night
Would we live to see the day

Remember we parked upon a hill
Was for this reason you know
To shine his coon light all around
The reflection we hoped would show

I began to wonder why I'd went
I could be tucked warm in bed
Instead of stumbling through the brush
With this coon light on my head

As the dogs pulled harder up the hill
Where we could get a better view
My arms grew tired of the steady pull
By then Dad surely knew

But like a beacon he saw a flash
As he swung around to see
That glorious truck just sitting there
Like it was supposed to be

When you're in the creek around a tree
Trying to find that coon
Round you go a lookin up
Your bearings you're sure to lose

Ended up, we weren't that far
From the spot where we had started
Got turned around in all the rush
We loaded up and soon departed

Family

As I look back upon that night
And lessons you can learn
Be prepared in all you do
And trust is something earned

We were lost but now we're found
No worries, cares or fears
Trust your Father to lead you home
And keep your memories near

My Dad

It's been 28 long years
Since I have seen my Dad
I miss his booming voice
Not having him makes us sad

But all things being equal
It's just your state of mind
I haven't really lost him
His memories I still can find

Memories are there to hold to
If you're willing just to try
We try to hold it all together
As the years go by passing by

Not having his physical presence
Somehow it's still the same
If you dig down deep within you
You can almost hear him say

"Talk to em", he would yell
When coon hunting with his hounds
He loved Rink, Roho and Judy
As they made their howling sounds

Baseball was his sport of choice
On the mound he was the best
An all-state pitcher from Taloga
He was better than the rest

He listened to his St. Louis Cardinals
By radio in the summer time
Harry Caray rocked us all to sleep
When Harry was in his prime

He was very stern disciplinarian
By threatening us with a belt
It wasn't just the one that he wore
The milk strap sure left a welt

He loved to farm and ranch though
As good with numbers as I've seen
Could figure the gain on the cattle
With expenses and costs in between

Growing wheat was his passion
It was deep down in his veins
Though work was hot and dirty
You seldom heard him complain

As a board member he has served
For soil conservation and the school
He was respected by all that knew him
Always remembering the golden rule

Of course he loved his family
His lovely wife and kids
Taking care of Pa and Granny
And Jess and Isie as he did

But one thing was most memorable
And I know he'd say the same
Is when he was in his sixties
He made a verbal choice to claim

Jesus as his lord and savior
And be baptized and submersed
By doing this it was settled
In heaven and here on earth

On where he'd spend eternity
And go on to just that place
To join the ones before him
And wait to see us at the gate

So if you haven't chosen
Jesus as Lord once and for all
Don't miss the opportunity
And heed the savior's call

A Life Well Lived

This year marks 95 years
In the life of W Jene Oakes
That's a long life in these parts
And the envy for most folks

Born in Custer county
Independence was the place
It's a ghost town nowadays
But it's memory you can't erase

She is the youngest of six kids
And the only one left today
There was Clyde and Gladys
Harold, John and Audrey Mae

She carries on her family legacy
With not even a first cousin left
With love and grace and dignity
In her presence we've all been blessed

Born in 29 during the depression
Work was hard in those days
You grew what food you ate
To look back we are amazed

Just think about the times she saw
And the struggles she endured
A young Mom picking cotton by hand
So the bills could be secured

Milked cows and separated cream
Cooked, cleaned and ringer washed
Raised three boys on the farm
And wouldn't let her dreams be squashed

Then when her youngest was old enough
She started a career at the bank
Some fifty two years it lasted
For her service we'd like to thank

She never took her family for granted
And always had time to bake
Her pies and biscuits were to die for
Let alone the rolls, cookies and cakes

Never once did we hear her complain
When us boys were still at home
About cooking, cleaning or ironing
With a smile her love was well shown

Now as time is marching along
It's our turn to clean, cook and care
For a mother that's done enough
Now our hands are willing to share

Though men don't have all the skills
Or trained in motherly ways
We had a great mentor to watch
As we care for her day by day

We are thankful for these years
We have shared with Mom without Dad
As his time was cut short by cancer
And those years we wished we'd had

But one thing is for certain here
An example has been well set
We all strive to be what she is
If we try we may get there yet

Uncle Jabe

He came to live at Granny's
To help with chores and such
He was my Granny's brother
To like him didn't take much

But he took a liken to me
Though I never knew quite why
But he was someone special
As I remember as years go by

I used to watch him whittle
On wood found on the ground
And listened to him whistle
Such a sweet and joyful sound

Of course it didn't take much
To impress a 5 year old kid
He took his time to teach me
And understand me like he did

Yes at 5 you don't understand much
Your life is simple at best
But to have someone like that
Take time and in you invest

He'd call me Kav not Kevin
Like my Pa would always do
He'd wink one eye so slowly
Then grin as he'd got to you

He'd make a swing from lumber
Hang a rope from the tallest tree
And swing me for hours on end
Just my Uncle Jabe and me

If you recall the Randy Travis tune
Talking about one he recalled
This was my Uncle Jabe
White starched shirt and all

So looking back on those times
So simple and free of care
Make a difference in someone special
And your time be willing to share

Mom's Shadow

Shadows are an amazing thing
And they never tell a lie
They are there with you each day
Until the day you say goodbye

As I took a walk with Mom today
"You cast a tall shadow" she said
"I don't recognize mine anymore
My how the years have fled"

We had walked this road before
Over sixty years have passed
Our shadows were much different
Images on the ground they cast

Hers was much bigger than mine
As I remember back long ago
"Your shadow will get bigger" she said
"But it will take some time to grow"

She was right, my shadow grew
Always telling the truth
It has followed me every day
And has been there since my youth

Though Mom's shadow is the same today
But now seen through different eyes
The years have shown a different view
A large shadow you can't deny

A shadow of a Mother's love
For her family and her friends
A shadow of her love of God
That will show until the end

A shadow of true faithfulness
Of knowing wrong from right
And teaching her sons the golden rule
And praying for us each night

Not a question in heaven or earth
When shadows are compared
Mom's will be among the best
And God has a place prepared

Now as the evening shadows
Grow longer with each day
Thank God for precious Mothers
As you kneel each night to pray

Uncle Harold

There are several times in life
When God shows you how to live
By placing folks in your path
To teach how to work and to give

For me that was Uncle Harold
My Mom's oldest brother
When he was around there was laughter
And he treated me like no other

A carpenter, harvester and farmer by trade
Always willing to lend a hand
Helped build my parent's home
And not afraid to take a stand

Living at Independence his whole life
That's North of Custer City a ways
Was a booming town in its early years
But the railroad went another way

He married a Pentecostal evangelist
And with two daughters they were blessed
With Edith they were taught the Golden rule
The Christian way as you would have guessed

He served in the Air Force in the war
And trained on the B17 bomber
To be a tail gunner was his duty
To serve with bravery and honor

Maybe custom harvesting was his calling
Following the golden fields of wheat
From the south to the north he'd go
Riding the combine was quite a treat

Was it being a carpenter like Jesus
Building things of beauty with wood
Or just being good with his hands
And fixing things that he could

He was a son, a brother, a husband
A dad, an uncle, a cousin, a friend
To know him holds a special meaning
Because he is faithful to the end

His smile is so contagious
His laughter envelopes the room
Always asking about your life
Never down or unhappy or gloom

His life then led him to the center
Where war veterans go to live
He rode around on his scooter
Taking time to stop and to give

98 years have come before him
He met each challenge as they came
With God as his faithful companion
Folks that knew him were forever changed

We will miss his smile and his laugh
The way he would brighten up each day
He has left a pattern for us to follow
A life of faith, love, hope and the Christian way

Dads

Time passes so slowly
when you're in your teens
Then speeds up quickly
As with age it seems

One day you look up
And you're fully grown
With a spouse and family
And out on your own

No turning back now
With commitments galore
A job and a mortgage
Like never before

Those days go so quickly
As life passes by
Kids are all busy
Time seems to fly

Grandmas and Grandpas
Are there with you too
With a helping hand
With so much to do

You wonder then
How they make the time
To be there for you
When you're in a bind

But they always were
And they had the space
In their lives for you
To make a better place

For you and your kids
Now looking back
With two of them gone
There's something we lack

Though two still remain
Both of our moms
Without those men in our lives
There seems something wrong

How strong those men were
In stature and pride
Both handsome and proud
And good on the inside

What a legacy they left
For us now to know
They both stand before God
With robes white as snow

Dad's Overalls

On this Father's Day
I try to recall
Little things about Dad
Sure, I don't remember all

But one thing stands out
Spring summer winter fall
His attire was the same
Blue and white striped overalls

Big Smith was his choice
Whether twas hot or was cold
He wore them each day
Til they were ragged and old

Family

I used to wonder why
But as I think of him I smiled
He grew up dirt poor
Wearing them as a child

Photos of him and his goats
Wearing overalls and no shoes
They were pulling his wagon
His destination, no clue

I remember after his shower
No sweats, none of that
He'd put on his bibs
With only one strap

Oh yes, he had slacks
And he had several suits
But when the style was casual
He went back to his roots

Yes, he had dark blue
And I mentioned the striped
I don't think that it mattered
He liked what he liked

There are still some hanging
In Mom's closet they're there
And as I go check my cows
This story I'll share

In the cool of the morn
On this Father's Day
I went to that closet
And you know what they say

The apple never falls
Too far from the tree
As I slipped on his bibs
I felt him smiling down on me

The Perfect Day

Sunday's, the last several years
Are different in a good way whereas
Taking time for Mom in the morning
Then on to church at Watonga Naz

Back to the farm with lunch with Mom
In the winter, feed the cows, look at them good
In the summer, mow the yard, repair the fences
And do the chores as a person should

Then when all is done and there's time left
Mom wants me to sing and play guitar
May be a tall order for some but not for me
A willing ear and a voice subpar

As I flip through the pages of my old songbook
Old dogs, children and watermelon wine appears
I always sing it and Mom comments
"I bet they don't even make that round here"

Well one day as we were shopping at the grocery store
I told my wife "I'm going to the wine section
To look if there is such a thing as watermelon wine
And I'm going to get it if there's no objection "

Sure enough, I found a bottle at the bottom
And I grabbed it with a nod and a smile
Wait until I show Mom next Sunday I thought
Folks thought I was drunk walking down that aisle

The next Sunday, Mom was feeling kinda down
But the look she gave when I showed her the label
"Look what I found" I said "Watermelon wine"
"Be back at noon" as I sat it on the table

When I returned at noon the table was set
Lunch was ready and wine glasses were out
We popped the cork and had us a sip
Tom T was right and now there's no doubt

We ate and we laughed and talked about life
And sipped our wine and weren't we a sight
We finished lunch then I had to go feed
"You want to go?" I said "yes I just might"

She got in the feed truck setting up high
Her and Dad spent their Sundays doing just this
This brought back memories as I opened the gate
These little things are the things that she's missed

We traveled back home and got settled in
I grabbed my guitar and tickled her a tune
Sang old country favs that she used to know
And some old pop songs like "Fly me to the moon"

As I finished my songs and prepared to leave
Mom always gets up and throws wisdom my way
What she said took me back in a humbling sense
"Thank you for making this such a perfect day"

The moral to this story if there's one to be told
It's the little things you do that matter in life
A simple jester of kindness is all that it takes
To make a big difference so don't think twice

Cowboy Days

We rode upon the hill, to scout out our next move
Our duties not quite over, still something left to prove
Should we charge full speed ahead, or retreat for just a bit
To get a better vantage point, on the hill now where we sit

The place was quiet and still, not a bird or cricket chirping
They too could sense the tension, of these Cowboys Wyatt Earping
You see we're all just Cowboys, we leave nothing here to chance
We stand for something bigger, not afraid to take a stance

When trouble comes a knocking, we heed its beckon call
We're the best this frontier has, setting in the saddle so proud and tall
With our badges shining brightly, hanging neatly on our chests
When we ride up close together, folks round these parts know we're best

Then the outlaws fire at us, each of us taking cover
We hid beneath the cedar limbs, making sure that it was over
We come right out with guns a blazin, knowing we could overtake em
And sure enough we were right, they surrender cause we made em

These Cowboys and outlaws mentioned here, ages 3, 6, 9, 13 and 7
5 in all, small and tall, our Grandkids are gifts from heaven
And the frontier that they ride on, it's our two acre farm house yard
Surrounded by red cedars, its perimeter these Cowboys guard

These cowboys and outlaws, come to play every now and again
And our yard and surrounding land becomes familiar like an ole friend
The canyon serves as a hideout to explore and discover old bones
Not from buffalo or from dinosaur but from the old cows that we have owned

You would think these were a treasure, from the depths of Mother Earth
As each grandkid collects them, no price they would be worth
They're excited each time the find one, it's a memory etched in time
Their discoveries never grow old, whether it's bones or rocks they find

But one thing is for certain, as they grow old and fill their minds
There'll be a place to come back to, to escape the daily grind
The farm house will always be there, as they gather from far and near
And recall their cowboy days, and these memories they hold so dear.

Grammy's Lap

What makes a child happy and comforted too
A joy to all around
What makes them all smile and snuggle and coo
Where happiness abounds

It's a place they all would like to be
Regardless of their age
At times you wish you had it
As life turns another page

When you have a scratch, a bruise or bump
When you hurt and feel down too
There's nothing like this place on earth
For burdens it can sooth

What is this place what can you do
To find this magical place
A loving touch, a big bear hug
With love and with God's grace

Others have never had a place
Or have forgotten what it meant
To have this kind of place
To most it's heaven sent

The place that's been described above
You can find as children know
When they snuggle into Grammy's lap
And start rocking to and fro

My Life Up To Date

I've had numerous people in my life
As I reflect upon the days
Have influenced what I am today
In so many various ways

First would be my lord and Christ
Cleared a path for me to go
With forgiveness and grace I don't deserve
His love He daily shows

Next would be my mom and dad
A guiding hand was given
With faith they taught me right from wrong
Those principles I'm still living

Family members were there too
Brothers, grandparents, uncles and aunts
All formed what I would come to be
As you look you can see at a glance

A little part of each of them
I took and made my own
To shape and form what I've become
Their influence clearly shown

But that is only a small amount
Of what has shaped my life
The biggest part of who I am
For 40 years has been my wife

She gave her love and made a home
A place of love, refuge and rest
When it came to the boys she gave it all
As a mother she is the best

Those sons have had an influence too
As they grew up and moved away
Now with a family and on their own
And living the Godly way

Our family has grown stronger
With trials, there's been a few
Maddox taught us about faith
And opened doors we never knew

Through that test like others before
Came hope and grace and love
Five grandchildren have come since that time
Each one a blessing from above

Now, it seems time goes so fast
My Dad once said to me
You're 25 and you look around
And your 60, how can that be?

Well, time flew by just as he said
As I stare at 60 nose to nose
Each day each hour each minute will come
And there's nothing you can do I suppose

But greet each day with a smiling face
So be ready when there's a need
God has a plan for all of us
And be willing as the spirit leads

Nicknames

Nicknames are used in place
Of your real name sometimes
I will try to recall a few of mine
And attempt to make them rhyme

The bow legged boll weevil
Was my handle on the CB
Or just weevil for short
Way easier to say don't you see

My uncle called me Cadillac
Why, I don't have a clue
But it sounds pretty classy
Probably would suit you too

Playing little league baseball
My coach called me Sandy
But playing make believe as a kid
I was always a Bobby or a Randy

Of course I was the southpaw
Because of my choice of hands
Being left handed has been easy
Something I'll never understand

In high school I was Slim K
I signed all my papers that way
I guess I thought that was cool
Some still call me that today

My brother calls me Kabin
My granddad called me Kav
Don't know why they felt the need
To name me different than what I have

But most friends call me KO
Or just simply O for short
I was called Taloga in college
Without knowing, was their last resort

I'm sure I've been called others
Probably won't name them all here
But Dad and Papa are my favorite
Those fill my heart with cheer

So you see I've had my share
And any of these nicknames will do
But Kevin works just as well
The next time I run into to you

But you can call me brother
And I pray you'll call me friend
Cause that's what we're called to be
And stay faithful until the end

CHAPTER II

Life's Experiences

Plowing

As a kid growing up on a farm
It was expected you learned how to plow
Back then there were no cabs on the tractors
Just a shade and the sweat on your brow

You learned the true meaning of endurance
You were let out at the field at eight
Picked up round noon for lunchtime
Was done when Dad pulled through gate

Those days you learned about working
About fixing things as they broke
Most farmer's equipment was older
Than today's farm and ranch folks

You learned about getting things done
As you moved from field to field
Your reward wouldn't come til next summer
As a good crop your farm ground would yield

That is if the elements would let you
Like the rain, the bugs or the drought
Regardless one thing was for certain
The plowing would continue no doubt

But how bout that dirt that was fogging
Into your eyes your lungs and your clothes
Tween the swatting of flies and mosquitos
We were having lots of fun I suppose

Now one time as we were a plowing
This fellow, I think Keith was his name
Gave me some Red Fox tobacco
I puked til I was almost ashamed

But most days round three in the evening
Pa would bring us a nice tall cold drink
Pepsi was his choice for those chosen
He would hand us and give us a wink

Now I'm not saying we were mistreated
For being out in the hot burning sun
For character was what we were building
Others reasons I am sure there are some

But I wouldn't trade one of those minutes
On a tractor, alone in the dust
For out of the dust came understanding
Of hard work, responsibility and trust

Seeds of Faith

I had hopes as I texted the words
I had invited three friends to church
My anticipation was high to see them there
Not thinking my feelings would be hurt

I waited by the door patiently
To greet them as they came in
Knowing I had made a difference
As the service was about to begin

We all began to sing
As the congregation gathered round
Seems the church was alive with spirit
But my friends could not be found

My mind was curious to see
Why my friends had been detained
Was there an earthquake or a wreck
Or maybe it was the rain

Or was it the crafty devil
Who is here to destroy, kill and steal
And keep my friends from the word
And to try to seal the deal

I had done my part in asking
And expected God do the rest
Thinking it would come full circle
Knowing I had done my best

But God's timing is not ours
And I may never know
How asking a friend to church
Planted the seed for faith to grow

The Cottonwood

In Eastern Dewey County
Along the Squirrel Creek bank
Stands a mighty Cottonwood
One of the biggest it would rank

It has mesmerized me for years
With its branches oh so high
Standing beside the road
It seems to touch the sky

I've always wanted to climb it
But I've now turned sixty three
Folks would say I'm crazy
For climbing that big ole tree

Just think of what it's seen
Through the many years it's stood
And the stories it could tell
If it could talk it would

It would tell of William Marlett
Of Texas Ranger fame
Come riding on his horse
To homestead and stake his claim

It saw Indians and pioneers
Horse draw carriages and cars
Kids going to school on horseback
And walking from near and far

From wagon trails to dusty roads
From graveled ones to paved
Through wind and rain and snow
Oh the storms that it has braved

My Dad buried his coon dogs
In a clearing to the southwest
Just beyond its outstretched limbs
A peaceful place of rest

Its trunk is twenty feet around
With no limbs for a ways up there
A ladder I may be needing
For my destiny up in the air

So I got the ladder ready
A drone photo would be good
The proof will come in handy
As I scale this Cottonwood

As I climbed, I thought of Knievel
Attempting another feat
I climb for the young at heart
And old age we're trying to beat

Once I scaled this beast
And seen what I had to see
Not an earth shattering deal
For a 63 year old to climb a tree

But one needs to recognize
The beauty that can be found
In the things that God has made
Just look, they're all around

I may never see the Redwoods
Or Ole Faithful I might well miss
But climbing this ole Cottonwood
I'll check off my bucket list

The Ride

As a small child you imitate
And want to be like your brothers
They rode horses gathering cattle
And I wanted to, like no other

After one such round up
They had penned all the cattle
They put me on ole Ribbon
Man I was tall in the saddle

Now Ribbon was an older horse
She'd been around for a while
But still had some spring in her step
Even after being ridden several miles

Now if you know anything about horses
When you give them the reins
Occasionally they'll head for home
That's what happened this day

But we were two miles from home
When ole Ribbon took off in a run
My gentle walk around the yard
Turned out to be not much fun

Now being small in stature
And not trained in horsemanship ways
I didn't know enough to pull back
After that everything was a daze

Ribbon and I did make it home
But didn't want to do that again
With one hand on the saddle horn
And never did grab the reins

There's a lesson for life journey
In my little horse riding event
If you've read this poem close enough
You'll see protection was heaven sent

And as for the reins that guided the horse
They were not a factor in this case
One, because I wasn't old enough to know
And two, I was a protected with God's grace

So when life seems out of control
And you don't know what to do
Pull back on the reins and listen
God will tell what is good for you

Leave the Light On

In our small country town
If the light is left on
At the funeral home downtown
Someone in our town is gone

Gone to meet their maker
Whether wealthy or were poor
The undertaker has turned the light on
Beside the funeral parlor door

Once this light is on
That person has breathed their last
No second chances given
This person's time has passed

Is your light turned on?
For the people you greet each day
Do they see the real you
In each and every way

Now's the time for living
Don't waste another moment
Stop by and see a lifelong friend
Feels kinda good now don't it?

Keep your light shining bright
Don't wait to turn it on
Your time will come soon enough
Shine bright before you're gone

A Youthful Encounter

It was Sunday, Easter morning
She hadn't been to church in a while
The church was having a breakfast
To be alone was not her style

She was greeted by two young men
Their ages were eleven and nine
Not the normal greeting party
But was arranged by God's design

"Haven't seen you before" the nine year old said
"Yeah, it's been a while since I've been here"
"You need to keep coming to our church
For churches in Guymon the choice is clear"

The lady reflected on years gone by
Because some how she'd lost her way
With the recent death of her husband
From church she was staying away

The boys were talking about shadows
Just like two youngster will do
"Did you know it's impossible to jump your shadow"
"Yeah, your shadow is always behind you"

That statement from a nine year old
From her mind she couldn't erase
You shadow is always behind you
God showed up, in that moment and place

Although her priorities had changed
And life had gotten in the way
God had never left her side
His grace was there in full display

She commented later on in the day
That statement changed her perspective
Not only can a pastor deliver a message
But a young boy can also be effective

Out of the mouths of babes
The Psalmist carefully penned
Using two sons of a pastor
To bring glory to Him

God's word can come from unlikely places
That's one of His wonders and joys
A lost soul has now been found
Thanks to the encounter with two young boys

A Transparent Observation

They drove past me
As I sat in my truck
I sat there proud
Like I had all the luck

As they got out I noticed
Their clothes were dirty and torn
Their hair was unkept
Their shoes tattered and worn

They both had cancer sticks
And their ashes were falling
As they walked right by me
They looked so appalling

I wondered to myself
How do you get there
To not care about yourself
How you look or what you wear

Then God's voice rose up
To love and correct
"I love them too" he said
"You need to love and respect"

His creations are all created
By Him and for Him
We all are equal in His eyes
My headlights were on dim

I felt ashamed and disgust
On how I saw those two
That's not the way I was taught
True feelings were coming through

I then felt thankful
For Him showing me what's right
To see through my dim view
With transparency showing me the light

If one day you are also
Looking down upon another
Remember God's word is true
And respect your fellow brother

Raisin' Kids

Being young parents you dream
Of what your kids will be
You teach them right from wrong
And wonder is that's the key

That will put them on the path
To be a great success
They go to school for years
You hope for all the best

And sometimes yes they fail
Though you thought they're tried and true
Raising kids is very tough
As your parents had once told you

And once they leave your house
You've done all that you can do
They're out and on their own
You worry you're not quite through

My Mom has a favorite saying
You'll never be truly done
Raising and guiding your children
No matter what age they've become

Whether they are 1 or 60 years old
You worry, you care and fret
As you know it does no good
But good outcomes you still expect

You expect them to carry your namesake
From here to eternity
And pass that on to their children
For all the world to see

When you get to be our age
And our younger days are gone
We have so little time now
To right too many wrongs

So teach kids when you can
While they think you hung the moon
And put them on the narrow path
Your time will end too soon

Plow Hand

Growing up on a farm
One thing that is expected
You learn how to plow
And do it as directed

Well as for me my teacher
Happened to be my big brother
He is known for little patience
But can farm like no other

This particular day it was hot
Of course it was mid-June
The harvest was complete
With the plowing still to do

The tractor was a John Deere
A 730 to be exact
Just a canvas covered shade
To keep the sun off your back

But being small in stature
And wet behind the ears
With big brother by your side
I had nothing really to fear

Was I in for a surprise
It wasn't as easy as I thought
The harvest had been good
And the straw was getting caught

The 11 foot chisel would ball up
And man was it a fight
To have to pull up and dump it
And swing out to the right

But being left handed
I wanted to go that way
Brother would have none of it
He had to correct me all day

Needless to say the day was long
And brotherly love there was none
Just big enough to reach the peddles
And worn out when the day was done

Eyes were red from crying I'm sure
Cause I knew I was right
Or was it left, crap I'm not sure
But am sure we were quite a sight

But I learned a valuable lesson
From someone I've come to respect
I'm positive it wasn't his choice
To teach and stick out his neck

I am not the last one he has taught
Young kin folk came after me
Though the patience was still the same
But the life's lessons were for free

So if you need a young one of yours
That needs a life lesson learned
I've got just the man who can teach
And will ask nothing in return

DeLong Hill

It was harvest time on the farm
Was the summer of 73
Combines were in the fields
As far as the eye could see

Our trucks were seldom used
And where could they be found?
They're outside, in barns and sheds
Until harvest comes around

Dad's old red Ford truck
It's brakes were completely out
So I was told to drive it
He dislike me, what's that about?

There's a mechanic up Seiling way
Where I was supposed to go
To get the brakes repaired
Was there danger, he had to know

But I was sixteen now
And had no brains or fear
Would climb into that truck
My mission was made clear

The trek was eighteen miles
Through dirt and highway travel
Just go slow and take no chances
But on the highway things unraveled

On highway west 270
DeLong hill is what it's named
Just south and east of Seiling
A vivid memory it became

It's an extremely steep ole hill
And long I can testify
Slower traffic keeps to the right
And faster cars pass on by

As I topped the hill I saw
A wreck at the very bottom
The road was completely blocked
Couldn't stop, now there's a problem

Cars were all backed up
From the bottom to the very top
What was I going to do
I knew I couldn't stop

I geared her down to third
All lanes were blocked on right
So left to the ditch I went
What I saw was quite a sight

Folks just gawked and stared
As I went on flying by
In the ditch down to the wreck
Then the cops just waved me by

Whether dumb luck or simply fate
Thank goodness for those cops
God's hand was surely in it
He knew I couldn't stop

I wondered if they knew
And surprised by what they saw
This outta control truck driver
Or was it shock and awe

And today as I went by it
In my spine it sent a chill
I remember that faithful day
My adventure on DeLong hill

The Other Hand

I was born in fifty seven
And from what I understand
My parents taught me the right way
But I used the other hand

Some folks say being a lefty is evil
It's not the natural way to be
The world is made for the right handed
Do anything left handed and you'll see

Now I've been a lefty all my life
But I remember in the first grade
I'd get tired of writing with my left
So with my right a letter would be made

You soon learn you're different than most
When you do sports of any kind
You can't borrow someone's baseball glove
A lefty's mitt is hard to find

It has its advantages too
Lefties are closer to first
But you can't play second, short or third
Others say southpaws are cursed

But a lot of famous folks were lefties
Aristotle, Mozart, Da Vinci, the Babe
Einstein, Mark Twain and Oprah
Bill Gates, Bill Clinton and honest Abe

So I'm in very good company
By using the other hand
And by adapting to a right handed world
Righties, you wouldn't understand

Try using a pair of scissors
With using you left hand alone
They don't work very good at all
Frustration is something we've known

But I'm glad I'm a left hander
And a little different than the rest
As God laid out His perfect plan
Being lefty, I've been so blessed

Just Drive

What are you really doing
When you get behind the wheel
Does it make you feel empowered
Or is it really no big deal

I am out on open roadways
Mostly all alone
But sometimes driving others
Either near or far from home

Do you think about what you're doing
When you climb into the car
Does your mind seem to wander
Not really knowing where you are

You know your cars a weapon
10000 pounds of steel
If you don't drive it safely
Your fate and others you can seal

Is texting that important
And is a burger and the fries
It's called distracted driving
When from the road you take your eyes

I heard an ole truck driver
Say a statement to proclaim
For years of safely driving
Without an accident to his name

I just drove son, he said
Was the response he always told
Kept my mind only on driving
Only concentrating on the road

So when you're out there driving
Take this strong advise
Remember, "just drive son"
And save yours and others lives

A Hug

Have you been hugged today
Were you hugged yesterday
Have you ever been hugged
In the kindest of ways

A hug can be a sign of affection
It can say hello or goodbye
A hug can be done without spoken words
A hug can calm you as you cry

You can get one for special occasions
You can get one for nothing at all
A hug can say job well done son
I've had those I do recall

A hug can be very uplifting
When you have failed without a doubt
From your friend, your mother your father
Your brother your sister your spouse

A hug can say Merry Christmas
It can say Happy New Year too
A hug can be a cheerful gesture
When you're feeling all sad and blue

A hug can be very reverent
As you bow your head to pray
The Father's presence is with you
In that special kind of way

So be careful when you're out there
Living life day by day
Be mindful of what you're doing
As you go along your way

Someone out there may need one
Take that chance and so
Make someone's day a little brighter
And be sure you're last to let go

The Poet Minister

There is a gentleman in our town
That is respected here by all
His words are healing forces
And is a man who has a call

I call him the poet minister
His words are so very divine
Such a humble and caring soul
With words he's hard to define

This man has such a gift
And is a master of his trade
When words are read they're treasured
Like something God has made

And indeed it's God inspired
Every poem is like a sermon
He has such a way with words
As if his words are predetermined

He gives words of healing power
To those who have lost a loved one
Or give hope when land has burned
And praise for God's only Son

His poems are about "Your Bird"
And "I have come to preach"
"The Dark Room" and "Now"
And oh the souls he's reached

These are a few of my favorites
But there are so many more
Too many to mention here
And can't wait for what's in store

But don't take my word here
Please read his whole collection
You too will soon agree with me
His poems are near perfection

He is the poet minister
For what he does for Christ
Without being behind the pulpit
There's no value that can be priced

CHAPTER III

SPORTS

Family Tradition

Sports to some families is sacred
Be it football, baseball or basketball
Or any ball there in between
Whether in summer, spring or fall

I believe in our family it's baseball
Handed down the love for the game
From Granddad, to Dad to me
Though it's changed, it's still the same

And yes, from me to my boys
And from them to kids of theirs
And hopefully that love will stay
And the love for the game they'll share

But looking back my Dad was the cornerstone
That fanned the flame of this passion
That we can point to, to this day
In every shape, form and fashion

He was an all-star to say the least
In this game his Dad taught him
He threw the ball like a flame
He's practice til daylight was dim

His talent was getting noticed
Teams were wanting his baseball skills
They liked how he played the game
To watch him, I hear was quite a thrill

He played for Putnam and Taloga
And Independence time was spent
The after high school in college
At OSU and Southwestern he went

Then semi-pro at Hobart
Where the pro-league scouts hung out
The offers had begun to come in
He would make it there was no doubt

But if you threw as much as he did
It was bound to happen I guess
Your arm just seems to wear out
It happens to even the best

But his love for the game never wavered
As us boys will always attest
Late night radio with Harry Carey
His Cardinals he loved the best

So if you see one of his boys
Or his grandkids or one of his greats
Just know it's a family tradition
When one of them steps up to the plate

The Homerun

The time was early June of 22
It was already late in the season
The baseball team was doing its best
To learn and have fun was the reason

Isaac was just five years old
Some teammates were already eight
But that didn't stop him from trying
On the bench he would patiently wait

He did get to hit, as every player did
Sometimes only one time a game
He dreamed of a home run
That would be his claim to fame

He was three foot nothing
But had ambition, ten feet tall
He thought he could anything
He would do it good or not at all

He'd watch his two older brothers
As they did all sorts of things
In his mind he was just as big
And could tackle anything life brings

He stated to his Dad, "tonight
A home run I'm going to hit"
The third inning he was first to bat
His mind was made up, it was legit

It was coach pitch and Dad was the pitcher
The first pitch he fouled straight back
It bounced off his forehead with a thump
Now he was mad, confidence he didn't lack

The next pitch was hit down the line to third
But it went foul, one more chance
Was the next pitch going to be it
Determination was in his glance

The next one he hit to third base
The third baseman threw it too late to first
He ran as if his legs were on fire
And he hit first base with a burst

The first baseman got the ball
And tried to chase him down
The little man was not stopping
On to second, then to third he would round

The third base coach tried to stop him
But destiny could not be denied
Never slowing down as he rounded third
He then crossed home plate with pride

The home run was now in the books
Just like the Babe calling his shot
Isaac did what he said he would do
Memories like these cannot be bought

There are life's lessons to learn from this
Confidence, determination and never quit
Isaac has shown he can do anything
And we've learned from him, we'll have to admit

Through These Eyes

As she steps up to the plate
Her mind is racing to see
Is this one the best one to hit
Or will the next one be

She thinks about pleasing her Dad
She does the best that she can
She swings at the ball and it goes
But rolls foul as to first she ran

The next pitch is a strike
As down the middle it goes
She lets this one go on by
Strike three by then she knows

She strolls back to the bench
The game is over by now
She gathers her glove and her bat
And keeps her composer somehow

She knows how the game is played
But the skill is not there yet
This girl of ten is smart
It will get there you can bet

But as she approaches her Dad
She lets her emotions go
Disappointed by how she played
As the tears began to flow

The walk to the car was slow
As she cried about how she had done
It's only a game you know
You need to be having fun

Thanks Papa for coming
She said as I turned to go
As I reached my pickup door
My tears began to flow

I felt so helpless leaving
Not being able to ease
The pain my grand-daughter was feeling
Father would you help her please

This was only one ballgame
A blink of an eye you see
As I looked through the eyes of a Papa
And the pain only God could free

The Catch

As a kid of 6 or 7
With older brothers ahead
They were normally Dad's helpers
But one day it was me instead

On a wheat truck with stock racks
Some calves we had loaded on
To take to the sale in OKC
With a long trip ahead we were gone

It was late afternoon when we started
On old 66 we would go
Setting alongside of my Dad
Up those hills we would go so slow

But finally coming into the city
We saw the bright ball field lights
Of 89'ers stadium at the fairgrounds
Oh man it was quite a site

Dad said," after we unload our stock
Would you like to go to the game?"
I said, "sure would, let's go"
In overalls Dad wasn't ashamed

We bought our tickets and found a seat
Right behind home plate we sat
The crowd was few, the night was warm
It was exciting to see them bat

We sat and watched intently
As each hitter tried his best
To knock it clean out of the park
And be better than the rest

One batter hit a foul ball
Very high and straight back it came
And Dad made an incredible bare handed catch
That put all the major leaguers to shame

He calmly sat back down
And handed me the ball
A wide eyed amazed little man
I couldn't believe what I just saw

The trip home was uneventful
And I'm sure I fell fast asleep
Grasping that baseball so tightly
With another memory of Dad to keep

The Fork in the Road

Back in the day there was a baseball player
Yogi was his name and it seemed to fit
One of his famous claim to fame quotes
"When you come to a fork in the road take it"

What in the wide world did he mean
Or was there no meaning whatsoever
Was he just trying to make us think
Or was he just trying to be clever

One thing is for sure for me
When I think of the fork in the road
I clearly see God's pathway there
With the choices in life and seeds sowed

We have forks in the road daily as we travel
From birth to death in this thing we call life
Some roads lead to good things and peace
While others lead to destruction and strife

We may not know which fork to take
Whether the road will be paved, dry or muddy
We all must trust in the Father to guide us
Keep in daily prayer, read the word and study

With hills, valleys, washouts and detours
We may need to grab another gear
With faith, God will lead us through
So trust in Him and have no fear

Maybe Mr. Berra wasn't so dumb
When you let his quote soak right in
So take that fork when you come to it
But always remember where you've been

Let God and His Son be your co-pilot
And like Carrie said "Jesus take the wheel"
Put your faith in the ONE who is true
The ONE who saves, comforts and heals

Hardy's Boys

When October rolls around
In the small rural schools
It's not football that is king
Hard court basketball is what rules

And in our small country town
Around 19 and 74
A man stepped into our lives
That would change us forevermore

David Hardy brought his family
To our small community school
And for the next several years
He would shakeup all the rules

We had never really been in shape
Until Coach Hardy came to town
"You'll pass out before you die" he'd yell
As the bleachers we'd run up and down

He taught us to play defense
In the passing lane keep your hand
He explained next receiver pressure
Whether in zone or man to man

He'd send us to KU for camp
To learn the finer skills
We'd come back better players
And dreams would be fulfilled

One drill we did as warmup
As impressive as one could be
He'd whistle and yell "Kansas"
As the crowd would rise to see

He'd grab us by the jersey
And tell us what to do
"Don't make excuses", he'd say
"You'll be better before we're through"

Each player had respect
For his knowledge of the game
If no improvement had been made
Only you would shoulder blame

Very few games were lost
Our junior and senior year
With coach Hardy at the helm
The Panthers were ones to fear

As we look back upon this man
We are grateful and feel blessed
For his character and his faith
We know we had the best

CHAPTER IV

LIGHT
HEARTED

The Old Man and the Frisbee

The year was 1957
Whamo came out with a toy
Called this flying disc the frisbee
I had one when I was a boy

Nowadays this toy is nothing special
With all the electronic games to play
Boys don't take time to go outside
And seem to just waste their day

When we were kids we were outside
My brothers and I were on the go
Playing catch with a ball of any kind
Or anything else we could throw

I remember those days so vividly
And wish for those days again
To have someone to play catch with
Even now that we're grown men

One day my grandson was visiting
Staying with us for the night
I was putting up some tools
When an ole frisbee came into my sight

I simply picked it up and threw
And flung it hard his way
He calmly caught it and threw it back
Time for me and him to play

My mind was full of wonder
And it took me back in time
Back to my childhood days
Before my age began to climb

A game of catch and throw
A simple but powerful display
Of a time gone by the wayside
That's not exercised today

But for those few fleeting moments
And in my mind we still will be
Just two boys playing outside
A grandson the old man and the frisbee

Would I Live There

Kansas is the name of the state
Ulysses the name of the town
Is this God forsaken country
Or is this the jewel on the crown

You can see for miles up there
It's as flat as a pancake you know
Why would anyone want to live here
I am going to attempt to show

First off if you're in irrigation
Or you own a section of land
This could the place for you
From what I can understand

Or you might be a cattle feeder
Cattle are plenty and lots are full
The smell will take your breath away
And really that's no bull

But what about the oilfield
Might bring you to this place
For gas fields there's no lacking
With Ulysses as their base

But what if you're a cowboy
Would this be a place to be
Ride the wide open spaces
And ride as far as you can see

And what about the hunting
With the pheasant, quail and deer
None of these are lacking
When you go to look round here

Are there tumble weeds out there
And what about the breeze
Tumble weeds are plenty
And the wind it blows with ease

So could I would I live there
Guess I can say I could
With proper medication
And take it like I should

The people there are nice though
As folks everywhere are
But I'm always feeling better
When I am leaving in my car

The moral to this story
As far as stories go
Be happy no matter where you live
And be happy when you go

Only a Mother
Could Love

I always wanted to play and sing
And pick my ole guitar
But I was always way too shy
To really go that far

I sang in front of the school
Back in my high school days
But the curtains were pulled in front
So they couldn't see my face

But my mother really liked my voice
To most others it was just ok
So way back then I realized
Mediocrity was here to stay

I sang at weddings when was asked
But really didn't know why
I guess they felt sorry for me
For being backward and shy

There were those times when folks would say
Go get your guitar and sing
Even then I felt inadequate
Of the sound my voice would bring

I guess you'd say the phone won't ring
To say it's Nashville calling
Because they know the basic truth
My voice in not that enthralling

I sing my best, that's what I do
But one thing is for sure of
I have the voice that heaven knows
That only a mother could love

Isla's Grace

She twirled and she swirled
As she danced the night away
She had to sing and dance
Before the dawning of the day

She rode in on her fearless steed
The pony she called Nor
Like the one Ruby had ridden
In the story of the legend of Thor

This night would have to do
To become whatever she wanted
In this poem Papa was writing
And not get too disappointed

She can run as fast as the wind
But an actress she wants to be
But she must learn to like a taco
But we'll have to wait and see

She lights up the room with laughter
Not a stranger has she met
There's great things ahead in her life
God will use her talents yet

Her room is not the cleanest
Her closet is just a mess
But when it comes to friendship
Her friends call her the best

The curtain swing wide open
As she steps upon the stage
Looks down at the roaring crowd
As her life turns another page

Her friends were watching carefully
As she flipped her beautiful hair
When she sang a song she'd written
There wasn't a dry eye left there

Her voice is unmistakable
So pure and clear and true
She is brave, smart and gorgeous
A free spirit through and through

The crowd gives her an ovation
On the stage roses are thrown
She cherishes this precious moment
But my how time has flown

She climbs back upon her pony
And waves to the crowd below
And rides off into the sunrise
We sure hate to see her go

But she'll be back again someday
As fast as Flash it seems
To become whatever she wants
And dream the biggest dreams

Country Music

What happened to that music
That country so proud and clear
With that twang heard in their voices
Country music for us to hear

Songs of momma, trains and trucks
Also some love with hurt and strife
Songs of God, prison and drinkin
As they taught us lessons of life

That music is what I grew up on
One at a time 45's would drop
Listening as a child with Mom
Never wanting that time to stop

That music is not heard today
With the exception of a chosen few
It was good back then as I recall
Here's a sample of the few I knew

I knew Willie before the braids
And knew Johnny before Folsom
I said the music was good
I never said it was wholesome

There was Hank and Hag and Jones
Buck and Dolly and Porter
Tammy, Loretta and Patsy
Not necessarily in that order

There was Pride of Mississippi
Arkansas claimed C. Twitty
Strait hailed from Texas
And Vince from Okie City

A rap you'd never hear
From one of these all-time greats
Reputation was on the line
For sure there was no mistake

Allen and Garth or Reba
Bob Wills or Roger Miller
Sang words you understood
Oh and don't forget about "the killer"

So Country Music what's going on
Instead of Rock or rap
Let's hear the steel and fiddle
Instead of that hip hop crap

Yes, I'm probably too old fashion
In the style of music I've heard
But give me the Statler Brothers
And sing along with every word

Light Hearted

Try to Stay Awake

At our age during the winter
When the time has changed
It gets dark so stinking early
Our lives are rearranged

Instead of working outside
Like in the summertime
We set still and watch tv
Like the news or shows on crime

As the days get shorter
And there's way less sun
We hit the sack a bit earlier
For there's less to be done

We continue this habit
All cold winter long
And get used to the sleep
Somehow, it's just wrong

While the tv's still on
We snooze and we snore
With a warm fuzzy blanket
And our life seems a bore

Try as we may
To keep wide awake
The next thing you know
Our mouth is agape

I remember my Grandma
Asleep in her chair
How can she do that
With us all setting there

Well what do you know
Now I've taken her place
Leaned way back in my chair
With drool covering my face

Then when we awaken
To the laughter and the stares
At our age we just grin
Cause we don't really care

So one of these days
Then maybe I will make
The 10 o'clock local news
And try to stay awake

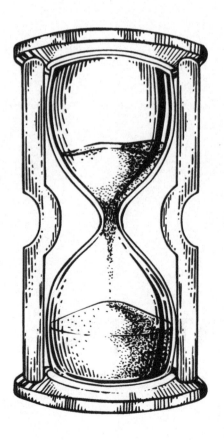

CHAPTER V

PETS

Abby

If dogs go to heaven
Somehow, we believe they do
God let Abby know she has a place
And we can go there too
Her life was filled was happiness
Not a stranger has she met
And when we enter heaven's gate
She'll be there you can bet

Baron

Our dog has left his footprints here
We're sad and a little blue
I wrote a poem at Abby's death
Thought Baron deserved one too

At first we didn't know him
As with our son he came to live
But their time with him was limited
Their pet they wanted to give

To us to bring back home
A dog again would bless
To be a faithful servant
Sort of a friend I guess

But he turned out to be
More than just another pet
He became a good companion
As on our lap he'd set

He'd eat most anything on earth
Whatever hit the floor
He once ate a 10 dollar bill
And still he wanted more

You'd pour his food into his bowl
He'd give the bowl a push
He liked his food outside his dish
For reasons we won't discuss

He never liked to be alone
He'd always throw a fit
But when we'd go he liked a treat
The dingo he never missed

He slept a lot throughout the years
As most dogs seem to do
At snoring he was masterful
The sound would raise the roof

His life was short in doggie years
Five years in human terms
His love he gave out willingly
Our respect he did earn

Sometimes God gives us time to spend
With others he does not
We need to make the most of it
Or have we all forgot

We all are just passing through
Like Baron's time has passed
His memories are still fresh to us
But like time, it's fading fast

So while its fresh I'll pen these words
To capture his life on earth
Remembering his wagging tail
And forget about the worst

Do dogs go on to after-life
Eternity to begin
I seem to think there is a place
Where we will meet again

CHAPTER VI

Whispers from the Windmill

Testimonies

The Hitchhiker
(A Friend's Testimony)

It was Sunday as he set in the drive
Loaded and his truck was all packed
He came home to visit his Mom
And not ready at all to head back

You see, his job was far away
And one he had really not chosen
Though he reluctantly took the position
And time was somehow now frozen

It was a very low time in his life
He thought that God had forgotten
With broken relationships behind him
He was lost and feeling so rotten

But just then an audible voice
Spoken from the Master above
"A hitchhiker you will pick up tonight
And learn more of my great love"

At once his gloom turned to excitement
And anticipated as he prayed
"When will I see him" he asked
He was willing but somewhat afraid

He would never pick up a stranger
But that was all about to change
He would trust in his Lord and Savior
With this hitchhiker God had arranged

The several hour trip seemed to drag on
But on and on he went
Was this again just wasted time
Did he misunderstand what He'd meant?

But along the road there appeared a man
As he approached the man he prayed
"Is this him God, give me a sign"
But on his heart nothing was laid

He kept on going, feeling down
Thinking he had just missed it
What blessings there could have been
In this pickup now where he sits

It was getting dark as he trekked along
As the two lane split to four
He saw this man along the road
His spirit was shook to the core

He passed too fast and couldn't stop
So on he went to find
A place where he could turn around
And not leave this blessing behind

As he pulled up he saw this man
One leg was gone to the knee
His crutches he quickly gathered up
And a backpack beside he could see

"Let me get that for you" he said
It was quite heavy to get up inside
"What in the world do you have in there?"
You could see the look in his eyes

"There are bibles in there" he said
"Always want to be prepared
Been praying for God to send someone
So the word with him I could share"

"Where are you headed" he asked
Not wanting to scorn or pry
"Springfield" he said, " is my next stop"
"Well good I'm going right by"

The hours that followed were precious
As the man opened up the word
And spoke words of strength and of glory
Like nothing he had ever heard

The word was straight from God
From the hitchhiker's mouth it came
To soothe a spirit once troubled
And to lift up the Father's name

It was exactly the words that were needed
In this man's heart and his mind
From an unlikely hitchhiking traveler
So insightful, caring and kind

So the next time you're feeling troubled
And you're struggling on what you should do
Know that God is up there listening
And He's caring for me and for you

God and the Big Mac

The world is a different place nowadays
You never know what to expect
As I pulled into the hotel
An old friend walked up that I respect

This chance meeting was destiny
I believe God had prearranged
Both our schedules to fit His
To some it would sound strange

We made small talk catching up
On our lives, jobs and such
Then parted and said "maybe catch you later"
Not thinking about it much

As I checked into my room
The lady at the desk said
"come eat with us tonight"
I had other plans instead

Spaghetti didn't sound good
As I needed to go to next door
To pick up a Mother's day card
At the local Wal-Mart store

In this Wal-Mart was a McDonalds
It just so happened you see
My mouth was all set for a Big Mac
But God had other plans for me

I got my card and grabbed my food
And headed back across the lot
Went up to my room and settled in
To eat the food I had got

Man was I hungry I thought
As I set across the bed
What I thought I got was a Big Mac
Turned into a fish sandwich instead

I don't know about you
But just the smell of fish
When you're expecting something else
Is not your favorite dish

So in the trash I threw it
And down the stairs I went
To eat the hotel spaghetti
Like it was heaven sent

As I walked into the lobby
Where the guests were gathered round
There sat my ole friend
I filled my plate and sat down

Again we made small talk
But God prompted me to say
"How are you and God?"
As we both were ending our day

"Funny you should ask he said
I haven't shared this story much
Let me tell you of an adventure"
As he talked I felt God's touch

Then my friend shared his testimony
That was heart felt and true
About him and God and a hitchhiker
That was meant for me and you

The testimony was powerful
And truly heaven sent
Written down for my friend
With intentions truly meant

So I wanted to tell you the story
How God turned a chain of events
Into something He could use
And what His love has meant

If I had received the Big Mac
There'd be nothing here to say
The words of my friends testimony
I would not have known today

So the next time that you believe
That God doesn't have a plan
Think of my fish sandwich
Then maybe you'll understand

Tell Them
What You Know

I am a simple thinking man
Not as smart as some others
But I want to share a word
To all my sisters and my brothers

These words are not my own
They belong to the Father above
He sends down His grace and peace
But mostly He sends down His love

He laid down His life on the cross
So we could gain our crown
We should be shouting from the rooftops
Through the countrysides and the towns

He arose from the grave
To accomplish His perfect plan
It's great news for all creation
Though we'll not fully understand

Until we stand before the our maker
The true beginning and the end
Then we'll truly understand
He has always been our friend

Yes Jesus died for you and me
All we have to do is believe
And ask him into our hearts
He freely gives, so simply receive

Once I was asked to speak
But did not know what to say
"Just tell them what you know"
A wise man told me that day

Someone you know needs to know
The Jesus that you know
God's plan is for us to share
From mountains high to the valleys low

So go tell that someone about Jesus
And do not tarry with this task
Our days on earth are numbered
It's such a simple thing to ask

So please pray before this journey
Not our will be done, but His
And simply tell them what you know
And what a perfect gift He is

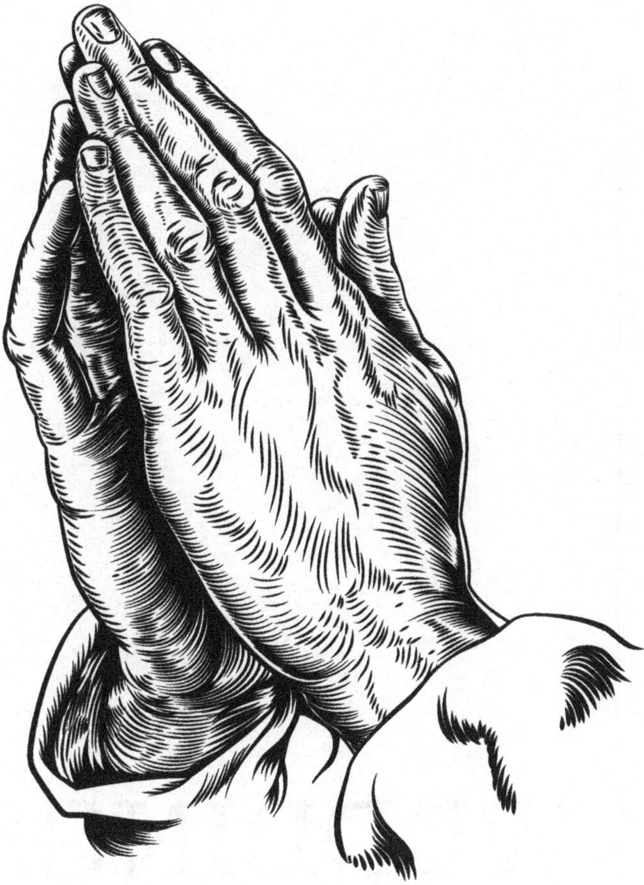

CHAPTER VII

WEDDINGS

The Cowboy I Found

You spend years looking for that special someone
Your hopes and dreams to share
Someone who's a lot like you
And would follow you anywhere

One who's kind and gentle and sweet
And can wrangle, rope and ride
Who's good with cattle and horses too
And would look good ridin by my side

They'd have to know how to clip
And get ready for a show
And even judge a show or two
And with livestock be in the know

And liking Herefords would be a plus
And be ready to do all the above
One whose faithfulness was unwavering
One who could know committed love

The cowboy life is a hard one
And not for the weak of heart
The days are long and the work is tuff
Each one must play their part

But these cowboys are good ones
And loves this cowboy's life
He will make a great husband
And she will make a great wife

Both can ride and rope and love
Both knows what all of this means
One looks great while in a dress
But really looks better in jeans

The commitment here is life long
With God's love you'll trust and find
This cowboy you have chosen
Is truly one of a kind

Our Story Begins

Once upon a time...
There were two bundles of joy
A pretty little girl and a cute little boy
Childhood innocence time passes so slow
Two separate lives as they continue to grow
Family was important when growing so fast
Let them be little, you knew it wouldn't last
Similar paths while attending school
Sports, church, music and the Golden Rule
Their paths finally cross, as fate somehow knew
This couple would wed and say their "I dos"
This story is not over, we've much yet to say
As the couple exchange vows, on this special day
But we'll leave you for now and hold back the tears
They will tell you the ending in 75 years

CHAPTER VIII

Faith

Inspiration

What inspires me is praying for a son
Who preaches the gospel or designs for fun
Or maybe it's a daughter who nurses with care
Or another who teaches about fitness she shares
Or is it a grand daughter who loves and who dreams
About what she'll become with no limit it seems
Or maybe a grandson with boots and with hat
Dreaming about horses and things such as that
Whomever you pray for be diligent in such
Because time is so limited, but the gain is so much
So next time you kneel, and ask God your requests
Pray for your family, and be amazed at what you get

Loved Ones

You know how you wonder
When loved ones pass away
Are they up there watching
As you go along your way

And if they are there watching
From the great eternity
Are they proud at what they're seeing
As they are watching you and me

Are they proud of how you're treating
Your spouse, your daughter, your son
Your co-worker or your friend
As each day is said and done

And I wonder if they cringe
At the things we say and do
And want to respectfully correct us
The way they used to do

And I wonder if they're proud
Of the way we all turned out
Of the choices that we made
And hope there is no doubt

Hopefully we can say
That we have done our best
With decisions concerning family
About faith and all the rest

Are we taking care of loved ones
The way we know we could
Or are we sometimes slacking
Not doing what we should

Have you called your loved ones lately
And told them how you feel
Or asked how they were doing
With intention that are real

What about the poor
Broken hearted or gone astray
Did you help when you are able
Do you know what you should say

I did help when I was able
I told them about the Christ
I paid for someone's groceries
I gave them some sound advice

If this is what you're doing
With your time each day and night
One day you'll stand in judgement
And say that you were right

But Jesus has the final say
For what you've done and said
You won't have much to say
Cause by then you will be dead

Your life will be over
No do overs are you given
But while you're still alive
Ask Jesus and you'll be forgiven

Loving Life

There's plenty of stress
As your life goes round
To be thinking sad thoughts
Much less writing them down

So it's my intention
Without sounding sappy
To tell you some things
That should make you happy

God has a plan
For you and for me
Jesus sacrificed his life
For you on that tree

Life's simple pleasures
Are always the best
The laugh of a baby
A good night's rest

Sing your favorite song
Like the star of the show
Songs like King of the Road
Or Baby Don't Go

Laugh out loud
When you see something funny
Tell someone I love you
Cherish days that are sunny

A playful kitty cat
Dancing just for the fun
Holding your grandchild
An early morning run

Breathing air after the rain
The rainbow in the sky
Freshly mowed grass
The smell of chicken as its fried

The love of a mother
The trust of a dad
Gifts from up above
Should all make you glad

A pat on the back
A firm grip handshake
Worship at church
What a difference it makes

Faith like a child
Living for today
Loving your job
Like there is no other way

Love your life
It isn't an accident
Life is a gift
It is truly heaven sent

The Days Gift

A young man had a wealthy uncle
Who was in very poor health
He asked this young man a question
"What would you do with all my wealth?"

Before he could answer the old man said
"I'm going to give it all to you
$1440 will be given to you each day
But there's a catch before we're through

You have to spend it all each day
Before the next day's amount is given
If you fail the money will stop
So have a plan and have a vision"

The old man eventually passed
And the money began rolling in
It was hard for this young man
Knowing what to do and how to spend

That's over $10 thousand a week
And $50 thousand a month
Could he keep this up forever
For anyone that's a bunch

This story should make us think
A valuable lesson it should teach us
God has given us each day as a gift
And each day He tries to reach us

Some will reach out to Him daily
While others will simply refuse
There's 1440 minutes in each day
It's up to us how they are used

There are no do overs or start agains
When the day is gone and done
We need to use our time wisely
Says God's only begotten Son

But one thing is totally different
Between God and the old man
With the old man, no second chances
With God, a salvation plan

God is full of grace and love
And it's for anyone who will say
"Lord Jesus save me please"
He'll never lead you astray

So have a plan and have a vision
On how your time is spent
Use your time to further His kingdom
And your blessings will be heaven sent

Calming the Storm

Back when our oldest was nine
The summer league was almost done
We were in the baseball championship
And storm clouds had covered the sun

Of course we were playing Leedey
Our friendly hometown foes
Seems we were both always there
That's the way the story usually goes

If you live in Oklahoma
When a cloud comes from the east
You knew it would be a bad one
Wind, hail and rain to say the least

I was one of the coaches
And I was wanted to play the game
But the clouds were looking bad
The closer that they came

As my father in law walked by
And said, "why the worried look"
I said, "the storm will rain us out"
And my comment was all it took

"Would you like for me to pray
And rebuke the storm from here?"
I said, "can you do that?"
He had no doubt and made it clear

He calmly walked over by himself
Praying Mark 11:23
Asking God to calm the storm
Like casting a mountain into the sea

Faith

114

The clouds obeyed at once
And fell down out of the sky
Just like that, they were gone
And he gave thanks to God on high

The power of this faithful man's prayer
With scripture belief and no doubt
Was able to calm the storm
Understanding God's word in and out

The game, so important at the time
Now seems insignificant at best
But God's word is true and pure
Thru time has stood the test

The Combine

It was another hard day in the field
As the farmer pulled up to the gate
There was plenty of work still to do
But most of it would have to wait

During harvest other work is on hold
Fields are ripe and ready to yield
What you've worked so hard to raise
As the combine is pulled into the field

Farming is an unforgiving way of life
You toil, you sweat and you pray
For the land to give up its bounty
To make your living each day

But it's also a satisfying life
Out in the wide open spaces
Breathing air that hasn't been touched
Or contaminated like so many places

But this day wasn't like the others
The farmer felt a pain in his chest
As he reached for the combine door
He just needed to set down to rest

He would never take another step
He fell dead face down on the floor
His heart had beat its last
His harvest days were no more

So they left the combine just setting
Where it was the day he died
Never to be started again
And it's not that they never tried

Faith

But the combine seemed to need
The masters touch to start
The ole farmer knew what it took
This info he'd forgot to impart

God is different than was the farmer
He has told us to be prepared
And be willing to witness to others
With the good news go boldly declare

So the morale of this old story
Don't let your combine set
Harvest souls as the fields are ready
This is one thing you'll never regret

Ole Cookie
and the Donkey

The wagon train was long
The Cowboys tough as nails
Ole Cookie was always there
On the long and dusty trail

His chuck wagon was loaded with food
Without it no one survived
It was important to keep him happy
If you wanted to stay alive

We simply called him cookie
But didn't know his name
He whipped up beans and biscuits
It all tasted bout the same

He brought along his donkey
As mean as one could get
Seemed no one knew the reason
But he had one you can bet

This stubborn little donkey
Would always pull back on the reins
His hind feet were always dragging
Behind the wagon train

So one evening after supper
We cornered him to see
Why keep this stubborn donkey
Why don't you set him free

He seems no good for nothing
He's always in the way
Without him behind the wagon
You'd have a better day

Ole cookie raised an eyebrow
Then slid his hat aside
He spit between his boots
Then spoke to us with pride

You fellers know bout the good book
Bout Jesus on that tree
How before they nailed him up there
For all the world to see

He came riding on a donkey
Through Jerusalem that day
To give his life for us fellers
There was no other way

I read the good book nightly
After fixin grub for you
It soothes the heart of many
God's word is pure and true

Over 140 times
As I read the blessed word
It talks about a donkey
Some things you've never heard

Like Samson who took the jawbone
Of a donkey as a weapon
And struck down 1000 men
Reckon he taught them a lesson

So my donkey is a reminder
Though he seems no good to you
Reminds me of the good book
And it's lessons that are true

So next time you see a donkey
Think of those things above
And know that Jesus rode one
And know that you are loved

The Power of the Cross

People look and study the cross
For a number of various reasons
It may be looked on at as a piece of jewelry
Or a decoration or a change of season

Let's look at what it should teach us
And what attributes it should bring
And the benefits found within
Not just an old hymn we would sing

The cross should teach us about sin
And how sin separates us from Him
God showed us His love while we were sinners
And without it our future would be grim

The cross teaches us about forgiveness
While Jesus hung on that tree
He forgave those that put him there
A great example for you and me

The cross teaches of success
His death may be considered a failure today
But when Jesus said "It is finished"
God's plan was completed in just that way

The cross teaches us about love
Greater love has no one than this
That he lay down his life for his friends
This is one lesson we don't want to miss

The cross teaches of Jesus' drawing power
He said "When I am lifted up from earth
I will draw all people to myself"
One cannot grasp what that statement is worth

Everything Jesus died for, belongs to us
The cross of Jesus is more than just a sign
It's proof of our redemption and adoption
It's the greatest symbol of love of all time

Webster can never completely describe
And history can never properly say
The power that was generated
From on that hill far away

Faith

Big Sky Country

The Montana sky was dawning
As he saddled up his horse
The day would be a long one
As the cattle he would force

Down from the hills
Before winter comes a rushing
In the wide open range
The cold will be crushing

He needed to rope and brand
Before that cold winter's day
And wean all the young ones
And send them on their way

This day seems a bit different
As he climbed upon the saddle
His life had been changed
It was no longer a battle

At an old country church
In the blinking of an eye
He gave his life to Jesus
And kissed his old life goodbye

The ole cowboy had struggled
For years about death
What would happen after this
When he drew his last breath

Would there be a bright light
Would you know where you are
Could I still ride my horse
Could you see near or far

These questions were puzzling
To the old cowboy for sure
Until he met the dear savior
And his heart was made pure

No longer does he wonder
About where he will go
The Bible tells us plainly
In its pages clearly shown

The grass seems much greener
As he rides through the plains
Not a worry in the world
With his hands on the reins

From his childhood he had known
A few precious hymns
He clears his old throat
And he sings some of them

As he sings, the sunrise
Peeps from over the hill
The cool morning breeze
Gives his face quite a chill

It feels good to be free
From sins deadly grip
And the worry he had known
From the saddle where he sits

Although the days will be long
Riding valleys far and wide
The load will seem lighter
With his Savior by his side

Why Am I Here?

Have you walked along the road of life
And questioned your existence
Why was I put here on earth
Here today and gone in an instant

Was I meant to do something special
Did He put me here for a special task
Or to touch someone's life today
These are questions I have asked

But before you get too far away
From thinking about your life
Think about what you've already done
By thinking of your friends your family and wife

You've done what is right
What is fair and what is just
You've worked hard to make a living
And to do the things you must

Have you thought about the little things
You aren't aware you do
With a smile, a gesture, or a nod
As in this life you are passing through

Those things make more impact
Than anyone can ever know
To those people you see every day
The kindness you are willing to show

So don't get so downtrodden
About why you're here today
Someone's day will be brighter
As you smile when you pass their way

The Bar Keep and the Bell

The cowboy rode up
After days on the trail
He was thirsty and tired
And hungry and frail

It was early on Sunday
As he tied up his horse
His clothes were all dusty
And were wrinkled of course

The saloon was nearby
He walked up to see
If anyone was stirring
It was quiet as can be

The bar keep was up
And asked "what you need"
"A drink and some food
And my horse needs some feed"

It's Sunday morn son
Need to change your ways
Won't serve the hard stuff
On God's sabbath day

I can offer you some milk
And for your horse some hay
Going to meet my family
At the school down the way

You're welcome to join us
As we gather to sing
And listen to God's word
Then they heard the bell ring

It was the school bell ringing
It was also the church
The meeting place for folks
Their heaven here on earth

The cowboy remembered
His mother's dear words
As she read him the bible
As a child he had heard

But he had gone astray
As men sometimes do
To chase down their dreams
So like a bird he had flew

From all of those teachings
His mother had taught
To do things he shouldn't
And remember he did not

Til he heard the bell ringing
His heart racing wild
The feelings he had felt
Years back as a child

The power of God's love
And the prayers of his Mom
Brought this cowboy to church
For some peace and some calm

The church doors were open
He stepped in and set down
The piano was playing
There was singing all around

The cowboy remembered
This feeling quite well
It showed on his face
As the tears began to well

His wild days were over
In his soul it was well
It just took the nudge of a bar keep
And the ringing of a bell

Custody Battle

He sees them most every weekend
As to his house they come again
He is so glad to see them there
He hopes for more time, but when?

These children nowadays
Have so much on their plate
Time with him is limited
He almost has to set a date

But while he has them he teaches
Molding and sculpting their minds
Showing them right from wrong
Being sure not to leave any behind

Faith

But weekends are so short with him
And most of those are only Sunday
What happens the rest of the week
And it all starts again on Monday

Because he knows the forces out there
Are powerful and relentless
Trying to steal what was taught
What can he do to prevent this?

He loves his children so much
And only wants what is best
He knows they have a free will
And he makes this one request

Please remember what you've learned
When Monday comes around
Keep me in your heart and soul
Set your feet on solid ground

God's the one in this custody battle
And He understands time is precious
He longs for us to dine with Him
To teach, discipline and bless us

The children he references are us
We rush though life like a timed test
Seldom slowing down enough to listen
To His voice and shut off the rest

Sundays are a fabulous day
To get refreshed and renewed
Praising Him and hearing His word
And reflecting on the week in review

Don't let Satan get a foothold
To steal your joy or your hope
Study and pray during the week too
So in this life you can always cope

If you find yourself in this fight
Slow down and listen for His voice
And win this battle for His time
You'll feel better and He'll rejoice

Joseph

Joseph was a man of God
Obedient, faithful and true
His soon to be wife was with child
What was he going to do

I'm sure he dropped down to his knees
To ask for guidance from above
An angel spoke to him in a dream
To explain God's plan and his love

Take this women to be your wife
Name this child Jesus
Not knowing that all along
That He had come to save us

Joseph done what he was told
As a follower of the Most High
Because he was a man of faith
And the God he followed wouldn't lie

The child was born and grew
In stature and in faith
Joseph kept a watchful eye
Full of love and care and grace

Not much is said in scripture
About Joseph after the temple event
When Jesus stayed behind
He was assured He was heaven sent

But Jesus was taught a trade
Working beside his dad He'd stay
Making a living as a carpenter
A humble and honorable trade

Later known as the carpenter's son
I'm sure Joseph was so proud
Guiding this young man of God
Long before He would draw a crowd

When my earthly journey is done
And I've said my last goodbyes
I'd like to visit with this man, Joseph
And look him squarely in the eye

And shake his hand and thank him
For being an example to his son
And for helping our Lord Jesus
And for being God's chosen one

And for setting the example for us
And listening to that still small voice
Having enough faith to respond
Then making the spiritual choice

Extended Warranty

We live in a time nowadays
Where there is division and doubt
We are bombarded with phone calls
Telling us our extended warranty has ran out

When in fact we may not still own the car
Or we never bought one in the first place
They continue to remind us with their calls
And keep pushing it in front of our face

Despite all the distractions in this life
There is good news for me and you
There's no need to pay for a warranty
When the struggles in our life are through

God has paid the bill in full
By sending His son and on that cross
Our extended warranty was paid
So not one single soul would ever be lost

All we have to do is answer the call
One call you really will want to take
By missing it or hanging up
Will be a huge eternal mistake

Our extended warranty is beyond this life
And extends from now until forever
Death is definitely not the end
Whatever your status, goal or endeavor

Someone you know, needs to know what you know
Our pastor continuously repeats
We need to shout it from the roof tops
In every country road and every city street

Faith

One person telling another
God doesn't have a plan B
There isn't any other way
God's perfect plan is you and me

The Resume

Good day Sir, it's Kevin
For a position I wanted to apply
Just to make sure you received it
Before my appointed time to die

I know you have gone on before
To prepare a place just for me
And I really don't need to apply
What you've laid out is free

I have taken the first step Sir
And accepted your Son as Savior
Watched my children do the same
Done my best to correct their behavior

Tried to be a good husband
Done my best to be a good friend
Though have fallen short most days
Still attempted to not offend

Sir, I have had sixty six years
Of life's experiences up to now
No sir, I don't believe I'm done
There are many rows left to plow

I've learned from those experiences
And passed that knowledge on down
To my kids and on to theirs
So they may one day wear a crown

My education has been from you
Attending church while just a pup
Studying and reading your words
Gone through life while looking up

All my skills have been given by you
Sir, I thank you, I've been blessed
Though not always used for your glory
Most of the time I've tried my best

For references, there are a few
To those that have had my back
Mom, Dad, Brothers, friends
My wife, my boys, faith never cracked

So God please accept this resume
And fill in where I have missed
And grant me a spot in heaven
Cause it's tops on my bucket list

Whispers From
The Windmill

The windmill stands alone
On a baron ole hill
To catch the flowing breeze
Many a tank it has filled

Faith

Oh the changes it has seen
As generations go on by
With innovations now known
You can ask yourself why

Why keep this ole thing
It's weathered and it's worn
It has been here for ages
Way before you born

Two blades now missing
And it creaks and it groans
How long will it last
And its future is unknown

Though it's seen better days
While performing its daily task
As with it and with life
Neither one of them will last

Like the windmill on the hill
We were put here for a purpose
You must dig deep within yourself
Not merely scratch the surface

The windmill too must go deep
For its life giving gift
God provides the wind
The windmill provides the lift

You believe you can lift the water
But you try and always fail
Many are the plans of the heart
It's the Lord's purpose that prevails

Whispers from the Windmill

When the woman encountered Jesus
As the Bible clearly tells
And He talked about living waters
Not given by the well

The spiritual sustenance provided
And salvation Jesus gives
Is shown unto the world
With the life that Jesus lived

So before your time has passed
Like the windmill on the hill
Say yes to Jesus' calling
So your purpose may be fulfilled

The End